KV-577-122

COVENTRY SCHOOLS LIBRARY SERVICE

Please return this book on or before
last date stamped.

Coventry City Council

SO MANY QUESTIONS about...
PLANTS

Sally Spray and Mark Ruffle

WAYLAND
www.waylandbooks.co.uk

First published in Great Britain in 2022 by Wayland
© Hodder and Stoughton Limited, 2022

All rights reserved.

HB ISBN: 978 1 5263 1779 7
PB ISBN: 978 1 5263 1780 3

Editor: Paul Rockett
Design and illustration: Mark Ruffle
www.rufflebrothers.com

MIX
Paper from
responsible sources
FSC
www.fsc.org   FSC® C104740

Printed in Dubai

Wayland
An imprint of Hachette Children's Group
Part of Hodder & Stoughton
Carmelite House
50 Victoria Embankment
London EC4Y 0DZ

An Hachette UK Company
www.hachette.co.uk
www.hachettechildrens.co.uk

The website addresses (URLs) included in this book were valid at
the time of going to press. However, it is possible that contents or
addresses may have changed since the publication of this book.
No responsibility for any such changes can be accepted by either
the author or the Publisher.

COVENTRY EDUCATION & LEARNING SERVICE	
3 8002 02120 128 2	
Askews & Holts	03-Mar-2022
580	£12.99

Have you ever wanted to know about plants? Think of all the questions you could ask ...

I have lots of questions for you.

I can help! Let's take one question at a time and see what answers we can find.

What are plants?

Plants are living, growing things. We can see them everywhere – in forests, fields, gardens and even in cracks in the pavement.

There are around 400,000 different kinds of plant in the world, and there are many more to be discovered!

From the tallest tree to the smallest floating algae, each and every plant is amazing and important to life on Earth.

Pop me in that pot, would you? I'm getting the urge to grow ...

Tree

Vines

Herbs

Roots

Bulb   Seed

Vegetables

Think about ... the plants around you.

4

Branch

Sun

Crops

Wheat

Sweetcorn

Barley

Oats

Bush

Poppies

Dandelion

Orchid

Rose

Shrub

Grasses

Ferns

Stem

Moss

Green algae

What plants can you see around you right now?
Do you have a favourite plant?
How would you describe it?

How many plants can you name?
Which plant do you want to find out about?
Have you ever planted a seed?

5

Do plants eat?

Plants don't eat but they do need food. Since they stay in the same place, they need to make their own food. Here's how they do it.

Plants make food through a process called **photosynthesis**. This happens in the leaves. They are the plants' food factories.

Each leaf uses energy from sunlight to convert water, nutrients and carbon dioxide gas into sugary food.

Carbon dioxide is absorbed by the leaves.

Flower

Leaf

Stem

A green chemical called **chlorophyll** soaks up energy from sunlight and makes leaves green.

Roots suck water and nutrients up from the ground and send them to all parts of the plant.

Roots

Think about ... how plants make their own food.

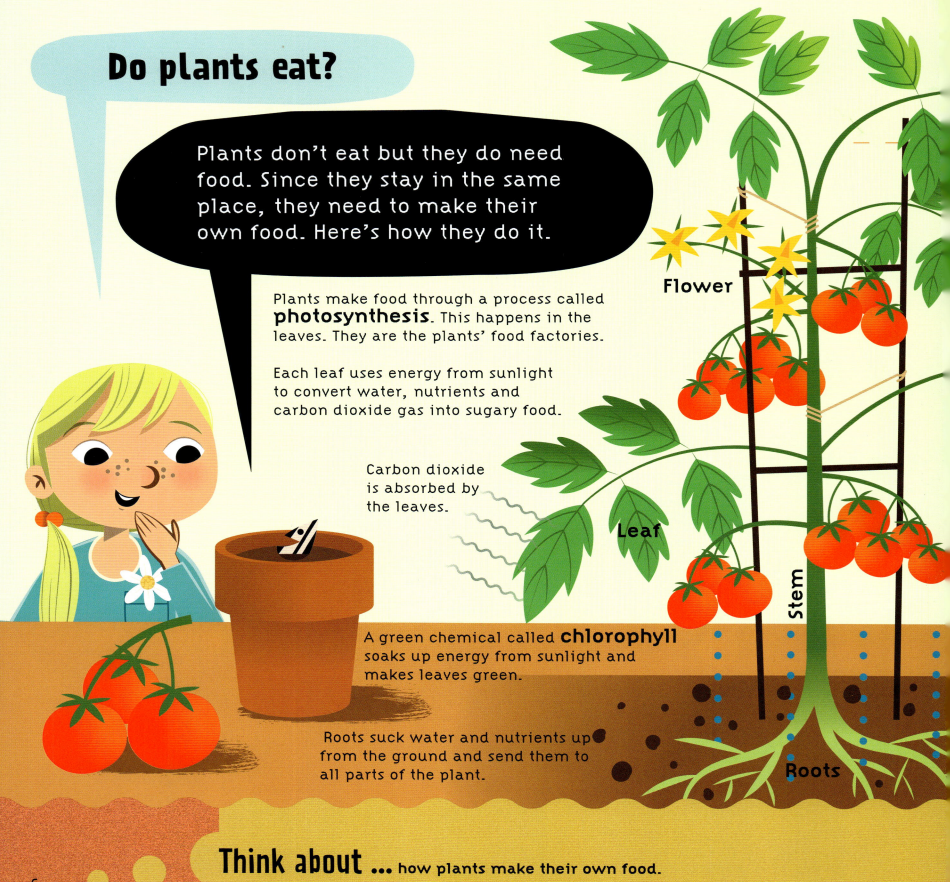

Water escapes through tiny holes in the underside of each leaf.

Sunlight

Water

Oxygen

Carbon dioxide

During photosynthesis, the leaves release oxygen, which is useful because that's what animals need to breathe.

Plants are so important. They take in carbon dioxide, release oxygen, provide homes for animals and become food for them too.

Fruit ← **Seed**

Carnivorous plants

Venus flytrap

Some plants have adapted to include insects and rodents in their diet. The animals are attracted by the sweet, sticky liquid made by the plants.

Pitcher plant

Hmm, I need a drink right now.

Why do plants make seeds?
Have you seen any carnivorous plants?

How do plants grow in deserts?
Why are plants so important for life on Earth?

How do new plants grow?

A seed has all the information it needs to make a new plant and some food to get growing. It needs warmth and water to germinate.

From seed to plant

1 The seed absorbs water and it swells up. Roots appear first and grow down.

2 A tiny shoot comes out and makes its way to the light.

3 Leaves grow from the shoot and start making food for the plant. More roots grow to find water and anchor it in the ground.

4 The plant keeps growing, producing new leaves and strong roots.

5 Flower buds start to develop.

6 These colourful flowers make sweet nectar to attract pollinating insects.

7 The flowers are replaced by tiny fruit, which contain seeds for future plants.

8 The fruit develops. It may be eaten, or drop to the ground to rot and release seeds ready to grow next year.

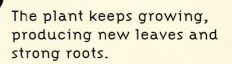

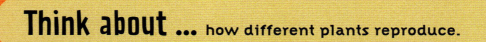

Think about ... how different plants reproduce.

Not all plants grow from seeds.

Some plants, including ferns and mosses, don't flower. They grow **spores** on their leaves.

The spores get carried away on the breeze, or by rain, to settle somewhere else and grow into clones of the parent plant.

Some plants grow from a bulb or from **tubers**. The eyes on this potato tuber are growing roots and shoots.

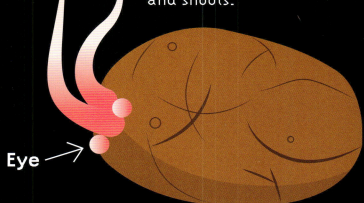

Eye

Rhizomes are chunky stems that grow outwards to produce new stems from which roots and leaves will sprout.

Strawberry fruit have seeds on the outside but the plants also grow runners, which are long stems. From the runners, new plants grow.

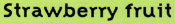

Gardeners grow some plants from **bulbs**.

Cuttings can be made from some plants. You cut a healthy shoot, plant it and hope it will grow roots.

Oooh, here come my roots!

Which of these plants would you like to grow?
What do all plants need to grow?

Why do some plants want to attract insects?
Why do plants make so many seeds?

Do animals and plants need each other?

Yes! Plants and animals are all linked by what eats what in food chains and food webs. Without plants, there would be no life on Earth.

Some animals help to scatter seeds.

Bright, tasty fruits attract animals to eat them. The plant needs the animals to eat the fruit and poop out the seeds in a new place where its seeds can grow into new plants.

Some seeds are carried on the wind.

Worms, snails and beetles are **decomposers**. They eat dead and rotting leaves and plants. This helps to break them down and recycle the goodness locked up inside.

Think about ... how plants and animals are linked.

Insects and birds drink the sweet nectar hidden in the middle of a flower. Pollen from the male parts of the flower sticks to the animals. When they land on the next flower, some of this pollen brushes off on the flower's female parts. This fertilises the flower, allowing it to make fruit and seeds.

Animals use plants and trees for shelter, for cosy dens to sleep in, and as safe places to build nests for their young.

Other seed pods open and release their seeds into the air or explode when they get wet, like the many-root.

Burrs are seed pods covered with tiny hooks that attach to passing furry creatures. Eventually the burrs drop off.

I've got a stem and two leaves. Now I'm a seedling!

What animals have you seen living in trees? How do earthworms help plants to grow?

How many different ways can you see animals helping plants on these pages?

11

Why do some trees lose their leaves?

Deciduous trees shed their leaves in autumn because the leaves are no longer useful. As the days get shorter and colder, trees store chlorophyll in their roots, saving it for next year. With no chlorophyll to make them green, leaves change colour to yellow, red and brown.

In winter a deciduous tree looks like a skeleton, with bare branches. It survives winter by resting until warmer days return.

Think about ... trees through the seasons.

Evergreen trees have waxy leaves that protect the leaves from heat and cold.

In spring the tree bursts into life. New roots grow below the ground to support new growth above. Buds burst into flowers and leaves begin to open and produce food.

In summer when the days are long and there may not be so much rain, trees start to slow down their outward growth, storing food and energy for colder days ahead. Some energy is used to make fruit and seeds, and the buds for next year's leaves.

Conifers have small pointy-shaped leaves called needles. The trees' shape allows snow to slide off its branches.

The **coconut palm** is a tropical evergreen. Lines of leaves, called fronds, grow out from the uppermost stems. The fronds are thick and flexible.

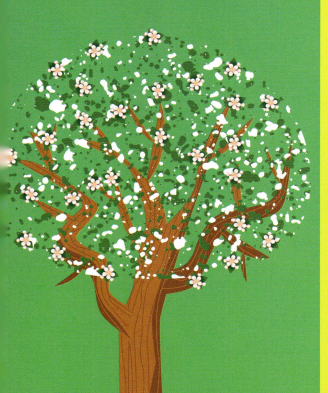

I'm so tall! Will I be a tree?

There are about **3 trillion trees** in the world right now. To combat climate change we need to protect trees, restore forests and plant a trillion more of the right trees in the right places.

Do you have a favourite tree? What makes it special? Which trees have the most vivid colours in autumn?

How can you get involved with tree-planting projects in your local area?

Why are flowers so colourful?

Bright flower petals attract pollinating animals, especially insects. The flowers of wind-pollinated plants, such as grasses, are small and green. They don't need to attract insects.

Bees can see purple flowers more clearly than flowers of other colours. Lavender is a good plant to grow if you want to support bees. Don't pull up other flowers though, as bees will still visit them!

Jasmine

Flowers also use scent, because insects can smell flowers before they can see them. Some flowers, including jasmine, release more scent as night falls to attract nocturnal moths.

Think about ... flowering plants and their colours.

Hummingbirds and **heliconias** rely on each other – the bird needs the flower for food, the flower needs the bird for pollination. This relationship works well, but would be in trouble if the bird or the flower disappeared.

The flower is long and slender to fit the bird's beak.

Broccoli and **cauliflower** are actually flowers.

You can also eat **nasturtium** and **pansy** flowers.

The tallest flower in the world is the **titan arum.** Its flower spike can reach 3 m. It attracts pollinating flies with its pongy smell.

The amazing **Puya Raimondii** is 15 m tall. Its stem can have up to 20,000 small flowers. It grows slowly and can take 28 years to flower!

I've got a bud!

Which of the flowers on this page is your favourite? Why? Why are insects so important to flowers?

Do you have space to grow some flowers that support pollinating insects?

15

How do we use plants?

People use plants in so many ways every day. Read on to find out about some of them.

Fruits such as blueberries, bananas and tomatoes are good to eat.

Leafy vegetables such as spinach and lettuce make tasty salads.

Root vegetables including carrots, potatoes and cassava are tasty roasted, boiled or mashed.

Nuts such as hazelnuts and chestnuts are healthy foods.

We use **grains** such as wheat, barley and rye to make bread.

Beans and peas are a good source of protein.

Different types of **seaweed** are used in cooking and made into fertiliser.

Sugar cane is made into **sugar**.

Cooking oils are made from plants such as olives, sunflower seeds and rapeseed.

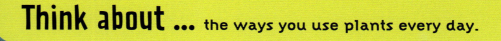

Think about ... the ways you use plants every day.

Farm animals eat **grass.**

Wood from trees is used to build houses and make furniture.

An average **tree** could be made into 170,000 pencils.

Wood from some trees is used to make sheets of paper.

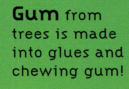

Gum from trees is made into glues and chewing gum!

GLUE

In Sumatra, Java and parts of India people make living bridges by training tree roots to grow across rivers.

Cotton fabric is spun from fluffy cotton fibres found inside cotton seed pods.

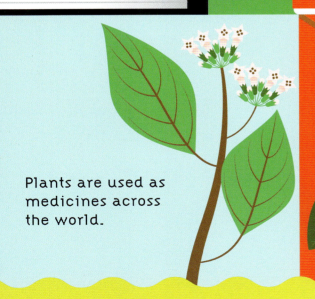

Plants are used as medicines across the world.

Sweet smelling **plant oils** like lavender and jojoba are used in soap, shampoo and perfumes.

Maybe I'll be a vegetable.

Which are your favourite plant foods? Which are your least favourite plant foods? Can you think of more ways we use plants?

Does your family use herbs and spices to flavour the food you eat? Find out which part of a plant they come from.

Do plants grow underwater?

Yes! Oceans, rivers and lakes are teeming with plant life, from tiny phytoplankton to towering kelp forests. Together they release at least 50 per cent of Earth's oxygen.

Water lilies have floating flowers and leaves and underwater stems and roots. The giant waterlily lives in the Amazon basin. Its huge circular leaves can support the weight of birds, such as this great egret.

Mangrove trees live along tropical estuaries and coasts. They are the only species of tree that can live in salty water. Their roots provide hiding places for young fish and help stop land from being washed away.

Think about ... the variety of underwater plants.

18

Phytoplankton are tiny plants, too small to see with the naked eye but very numerous. They release oxygen into the water and are at the bottom of every ocean food chain.

Seagrasses grow in shallow waters on coastlines from the tropics to the Arctic Circle. They help feed and shelter fish, crabs and seahorses. They have roots and even flowers that are pollinated by tiny shrimps called amphipods.

Kelp is a type of seaweed. It grows in huge forests in cool seas and supports a great variety of wildlife.

Why are water plants so important?
What do people use seaweed for?

What plants have you seen along the coast?

Can trees talk?

Not like you do, but they can communicate with each other through a fungal network underground.

A special fungi grow around and inside the roots of trees. Trees feed the fungi with sugars and the fungi give the trees nutrients.

The fungi grow to form a network of long underground strands. Trees use this fungal network to send messages and share food with each other. It is called the **Wood Wide Web.**

An older tree, called a mother tree, will send food to its nearby seedlings to help them grow.

Think about ... what plants might say to each other.

A dying plant or tree can send its store of food and nutrients into the fungal network to be used by other plants.

So you see, some plants have a secret way of communicating.

If a plant is attacked by insects, it can alert its neighbours so that they increase their defences.

Some plants give off chemicals that harm nearby plants. The golden marigold and the black walnut tree do this.

Why do you think fungi and trees help each other using the Wood Wide Web?

If people chop down forests, what will happen to the Wood Wide Web?

What amazing plant facts can you tell me?

All plants are amazing! Here are some especially exciting facts.

Snowdrops flower even when it's snowing.

The tallest trees are **redwoods**. The tallest of all is called Hyperion and it's 115 m tall. Redwoods can live for over 2,000 years.

Cherry blossoms are celebrated in Japan. People gather to sit under the trees eating picnics and watching the short-lived beauty of the pink flowers.

Think about ... different weird and wonderful plants.

Air plants grow on other plants and trees, and gather moisture and nutrients from the air.

Strawberries are the only fruit to have seeds on the surface. There are about 200 seeds on each strawberry!

The **acacia tree** is home to the acacia ant, which will attack anything that touches the tree.

Nettles are covered in hollow hairs that inject toxins into skin.

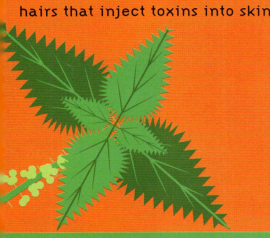

Lithops are camouflaged amongst the stones where they grow. Some look like tiny brains and others like small spotty bottoms!

The **barrel cactus** is covered with large spines to stop animals from eating it.

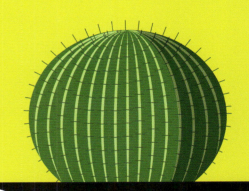

Cacti have roots that spread over a wide area to absorb rainfall when it happens. They store it in their stems. The tallest cactus on record was over 23 m tall. The smallest, *Blossfeldia liliputana*, is just 12 mm across. It looks like a tiny stone until a flower pops open.

I'm flowering! I'm a gorgeous sunny, sunflower!

Find out: where do redwoods grow in great numbers?

What is the most amazing plant fact that you know?

Are plants good for you?

Eating plenty of fruit and vegetables is really good for you but being around plants is good for your mind and mood as well.

When you run about or spend time in green spaces, you brain releases chemicals that help to calm your mind and make you feel happier.

Some scientists think that chemicals released by plants improve your immune system when you breathe them in.

Being surrounded by plants can make you feel **happy and relaxed**.

Think about ... how green spaces make you feel.

I hope I make people happy. That bee is tickling me!

Plants can help reduce stress by lowering your heart rate and reducing worries.

Plants can engage all your **senses** – sight, sound, smell, touch and taste.

Being in green spaces improves **mood** and boosts **self-esteem**.

Plants can **inspire** people to think of new ideas.

Green can make you feel different **emotions**. The fresh green of new growth feels inspiring, while darker greens feel cosy and safe.

Gardening, growing and tending plants is **good exercise** and is relaxing.

Gardening **increases concentration**, attention and memory.

Do you feel different after you've spent time outdoors in a garden, park or wild place?

How does it make you feel when you see a seed start to grow into a plant? Keep a growing diary and also record your feelings.

What is the future for plants?

Plant protection

We need to protect wild places from forest fires, floods and other effects of climate change.

Plants for all

Continue to investigate ways to farm for the benefit of everyone.

New medicine discoveries

Discover new plants that can cure disease.

Eco buildings

Build more eco homes, using natural resources such as wood and straw.

Think about ... what you've learnt about plants.

Greener cities

Plant more trees and other plants in cities to lower pollution, grow more food and help combat climate change. Improve the environment with beautiful green parks, walls and roof gardens.

Powerful plants

Support more research into how plants could be used to make energy.

My future is in all the seeds I've got. Will you plant some more next year?

Save disappearing plants

People are already saving seeds in seed banks around the world, and we need to continue to save the seeds of endangered plants. If some plants disappear, animals that rely on them may disappear too.

Eat your greens

Eat more plants — it's good for you and the environment. Waste less food.

It's over to you. The future of plants is in your hands.

Many more questions!

1. Can you see a plant right now? What is it?

2. What's your favourite plant in the book? Why?

3. What's the tallest tree in the world and where does it grow?

4. What colour flowers do bees really like?

5. Which animals graze on seagrass?

6. How can trees help combat climate change?

7. How many seeds (or pips) does an apple have?

8. What is a rhizome?

9. How are plants good for you?

10. Which plants are a source of protein?

Further information

Websites

www.croptrust.org/our-work/svalbard-global-seed-vault/

www.kew.org

www.nhm.ac.uk/discover/plants.html

Books

Discover and Do: Plants by Jane Lacey (Franklin Watts, 2021)

Planting Peace by Gwendolyn Hooks (Wayland, 2021)

Plants Save the World by Annabel Savery (Wayland, 2022)

Glossary

Adapted – when a living thing has developed a special feature that helps it survive. Adaptations pass from a living thing to its offspring

Algae – seaweeds and tiny plant-like living things that live in water

Bulb – the underground part of a plant that stores energy in order to grow into a new plant each year

Camouflage – blending in with the background

Carbon dioxide – a gas in air that plants take in through their leaves and can store in their living cells

Carnivorous – eating animals (meat)

Chlorophyll – a green chemical found in leaves

Climate change – a change in the normal weather around the world

Crop – plants grown in large quantities as food, such as wheat, rice and oats

Deciduous – deciduous trees lose their leaves in autumn and winter

Decomposer – a living thing that helps dead stuff to decompose (rot), breaking it down into tiny bits

Endangered – at risk of dying out and becoming extinct

Estuary – where a river meets the sea on the coast

Evergreen – plants, including many trees, that keep their leaves all year round

Fertilise – in plants, when pollen reaches an egg cell, allowing it to start developing into a new plant

Food chain – the plants and animals linked together by what eats what

Food web – the food chains linked together by what eats what in a habitat

Fruit – the part of a plant that contains its seeds

Fungi – living things that feed on dead material, helping it to decompose

Germinate – when a seed starts to grow

Heart rate – how many times the heart beats in a minute

Immune system – the parts of the body that work together to protect it from infection and disease

Nectar – a sweet liquid made by plants in their flowers

Nocturnal – active at night

Nut – a small hard fruit

Nutrient – something used by a living thing as food to live and grow

Oxygen – a gas in air that animals breathe in and plants release during photosynthesis

Phytoplankton – tiny plants that float near the surface of seas and oceans

Photosynthesis – the way plants use sunlight, carbon dioxide and water to make food

Pollen – yellow powder made by the male part of a flower

Pollinate – to move pollen from one flower to another, leading to fertilisation. It allows a plant to make fruit and seeds

Reproduce – when plants reproduce, they make seeds from which new plants can grow

Rhizome – an underground stem

Rotting – when something is breaking down

Seaweed – plant-like living things that grow in the sea

Seed – the small, hard part of a plant, from which a new plant grows

Seed bank – a special building where seeds are kept safe

Seedling – a young plant

Self-esteem – feeling content with your own character and abilities

Spore – a tiny plant cell that can develop into another plant

Stress – feeling tense, worried, on edge, as a result of pressure or some other threat

Toxic – poisonous

Tropics – the hottest area of the world, either side of the equator

Wind-pollinated plants – plants where pollen is carried in the air, rather than by an animal

Game cards

You can play with the game cards in a number of ways:
Choose a plant card and get a friend to ask questions that you can answer with a yes or no, e.g.
Is it a tree? They can guess the card through a process of elimination.

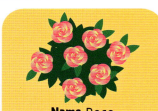

Name Rose
Description
Sweet smelling beauty

Lifespan 3,650 days
Height 240 cm
Varieties 30,000
Seeds per fruit 7

Name Fern
Description
Green leafy fronds

Lifespan 36,500 days
Height 180 cm
Varieties 20,000
Seeds per fruit 0

Name Venus flytrap
Description
Insect snapper

Lifespan 7,300 days
Height 30 cm
Varieties 1
Seeds per fruit 360

Name Tomato plant
Description
Tasty red fruits

Lifespan 365 days
Height 180 cm
Varieties 10,000
Seeds per fruit 300

Name Black walnut tree
Description
Killer tree

Lifespan 73,000 days
Height 4,000 cm
Varieties 1
Seeds per fruit 300

Name Sunflower
Description
Sunshine flower

Lifespan 100 days
Height 400 cm
Varieties 70
Seeds per fruit 1,400

Name Strawberry plant
Description
Heart-shaped fruit

Lifespan 2,190 days
Height 30 cm
Varieties 600
Seeds per fruit 200

Name Lithops
Description
Two stubby leaves

Lifespan 18,250 days
Height 5 cm
Varieties 145
Seeds per fruit 300

Name Banana plant
Description
Curvy yellow fruit

Lifespan 9,125 days
Height 365 cm
Varieties 1,000
Seeds per fruit 9

Name Lettuce
Description
Super in salads

Lifespan 130 days
Height 100 cm
Varieties 140
Seeds per fruit 25

Name Nettle
Description
A stinger

Lifespan 365 days
Height 120 cm
Varieties 40
Seeds per fruit 20,000

Name Potato
Description
Tasty tubers

Lifespan 120 days
Height 100 cm
Varieties 4,000
Seeds per fruit 300

Name Nasturtium
Description
Edible flowers

Lifespan 120 days
Height 30 cm
Varieties 80
Seeds per fruit 1

Name Conifer
Description
Evergreen tree

Lifespan 109,500 days
Height 3,500 cm
Varieties 615
Seeds per fruit 100

Name Cotton plant
Description
Fluffy seed pod

Lifespan 365 days
Height 180 cm
Varieties 52
Seeds per fruit 45

Some game card figures are estimated

Photograph or scan the cards, print them, cut them out and you can play the following games:
- Top Trumps
- Snap (you will need to print out two sets of cards)
- Lotto (you will need to print out two sets of cards)
- Matching pairs (you will need to print out two sets of cards).

Create your own plant cards to add to the pack!

Name Poppy plant
Description
Bright red flower

Lifespan 73,000 days
Height 120 cm
Varieties 70
Seeds per fruit 200

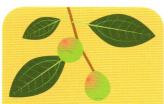

Name Jojoba
Description
Skin soothing plant

Lifespan 73,000 days
Height 300 cm
Varieties 1
Seeds per fruit 3

Name Sugar cane
Description
It's super sweet

Lifespan 3650 days
Height 700 cm
Varieties 5
Seeds per fruit 0

Name Snowdrops
Description
Winter flower

Lifespan 182 days
Height 12 cm
Varieties 44
Seeds per fruit 0

Name Air plant
Description
Doesn't like soil

Lifespan 2,920 days
Height 45 cm
Varieties 650
Seeds per fruit 200

Name Titan arum
Description
A stinker

Lifespan 14,600 days
Height 400 cm
Varieties 1
Seeds per fruit 1

Name Broccoli
Description
Eat your greens

Lifespan 730 days
Height 76 cm
Varieties 27
Seeds per fruit 30

Name Dandelion
Description
Fluffy seed head

Lifespan 4,745 days
Height 45 cm
Varieties 250
Seeds per fruit 1

Name Apple tree
Description
Favourite fruit tree

Lifespan 16,425 days
Height 365 cm
Varieties 30,000
Seeds per fruit 8

Name Orchid
Description
Beautiful flower

Lifespan 36,500 days
Height 90 cm
Varieties 28,00
Seeds per fruit 4,000,000

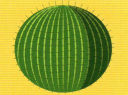

Name Barrel cactus
Description
Prickly ball

Lifespan 36,500 day
Height 60 cms
Varieties 19
Seeds per fruit 1,000

Name Carrot plant
Description
Crunchy orange root

Lifespan 730 days
Height 30 cm
Varieties 44
Seeds per fruit 2

Name Grape vine
Description
Fruit in bunches

Lifespan 51,100 days
Height 2,400 cm
Varieties 79
Seeds per fruit 4

Name Jasmine
Description
Perfume at dusk

Lifespan 5,475 days
Height 450 cm
Varieties 200
Seeds per fruit 100

Name Acacia Tree
Description
Acacia ant home

Lifespan 10,950 days
Height 1,500 cm
Varieties 160
Seeds per fruit 9

Index

3 8002 02120 128 2